Certification and Troubleshooting Fiber Optic Networks

Rev. 14

Developed By

Pearson Technologies Inc.
Professional Fiber Optic Training

4671 Hickory Bend Drive
Acworth GA 30102
(770) 490-9991
www.ptnowire.com
fiberguru@ptnowire.com

file: TSX_V14.0

1. Introduction

We have designed this troubleshooting text to complement hands on training using Professional Fiber Optic Installation, v.9 or V10, as the training text.

This troubleshooting text contains the following parts:

1. Instructions for performing the troubleshooting and/or certification of sample fiber links created by Pearson Technologies Inc.
2. Exercises for identification of curser placement on OTDR traces, as described in Ch. 15 of the text.
3. Forms for connector inspection, evaluation and testing, as described in Chapters 14, 20, and 24 of the training text.
4. A form for determination of the range of connector loss, as described in Chapter 5 of the text.
5. Forms for determination of acceptance values, for Exercises 19.1 and 19.2 of Chapter 19 of the training text.
6. A safety sheet issued by the FOA.
7. An FOA CFOT application form
8. An FOA CFOT examination answer form.

2. **Troubleshooting Exercises**

2.1. Troubleshooting and certification require the same activities, but with different starting points. For certification, the starting question: is the link reliably and properly installed? Troubleshooting starts with the fact that something is incorrect. For troubleshooting, the starting question is: where is the problem [i.e., high loss, broken fiber, etc.].

2.2. The troubleshooting exercises train technicians in the following aspects:
1. Calculation of insertion loss acceptance values
2. Selection of correct methods of insertion loss testing from the three types: HOML, EF, and singlemode
3. Calculation of OTDR acceptance values
4. Converting link maps to OTDR acceptance values
5. Making OTDR tests
6. Placement of cursers on OTDR traces for accurate measurements
7. Interpretation of OTDR measurements
8. Identification of locations of high losses
9. Identification of cause of high losses

2.3. **General Instructions On The Exercises**

The maps identify the end numbers of the fiber(s). If there is one channel in the cable system, the label will include only the end number; e.g., End 1, End 2.

If there are two channels in the exercise, the label will include the channel as a letter and the end as a number; e.g., 1A is end 1 of channel A and 1B is end 1 of channel B.

Treat all exercises as certification exercises. There may or may not be problems. Your objective is to certify the network as being properly installed, or not. Do not open the exercises cases unless instructed to do so.

Perform all insertion loss measurements by Method B, the one lead reference method.

2.4. **Sequence Of Activities**

1. Calculate 850 nm insertion loss acceptance values. Use 1310 nm for singlemode fiber.
2. Calculate 1300 nm insertion loss acceptance values. Use 1550 nm for singlemode fiber.
3. Calculate 850 nm OTDR acceptance values. Use 1310 nm for singlemode fiber.
4. Calculate 1300 nm OTDR acceptance values. Use 1550 nm for singlemode fiber.
5. Perform 850 nm insertion loss tests. Use 1310 nm for singlemode fiber.
6. Perform 850 nm OTDR test. Use 1310 nm for singlemode fiber.
7. Perform 1300 nm insertion loss test. Use 1550 nm for singlemode fiber.
8. Perform 1300 nm OTDR test. Use 1550 nm for singlemode fiber.

2.5. <u>Insertion Loss Review</u>

50μ @ 850 nm
Option A, Measure Input Power Level, EF Compliant Source

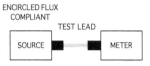

Option A, Measure Output Power/Loss

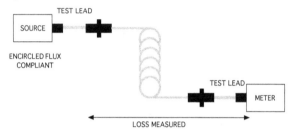

Option B, Measure Input Power Level, EF Compliant Test Lead/Mode Conditioner

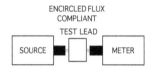

Option B, Measure Output Power/Loss

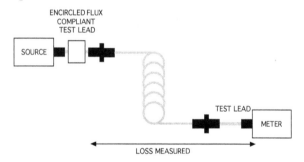

62.5μ, Both Wavelengths

Option A, Measure Input Power Level, 0.1<HOML<0.6

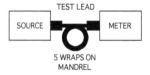

Option A, Measure Output Power/Loss

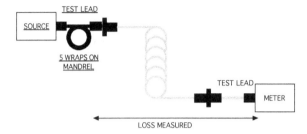

Option B, Measure Input Power Level, HOML>0.6

Option B, Measure Output Power/Loss

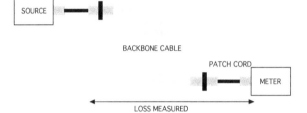

50μ @ 1300 nm

The measurement is the same as for 62.5μ, Option A

The measurement is the same as for 62.5μ, Option B

Singlemode, Both Wavelengths

Measure Input Power Level

Measure Output Power/Loss

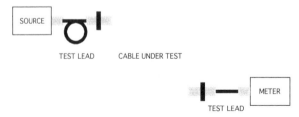

2.6. OTDR Module Sharing And File Saving Instructions

Each team will have a computer. An OTDR module will be connected to the computer as set up by the instructor.

OTDR modules are shared. In order to enable sharing, trainees are to shoot all traces for an exercise in sequence and analyze them afterwards. For example, a two-channel exercise will have a total of 4 traces. Label the traces in accordance with the following instructions.

Make a trace. Save it in the folder labeled "[today's date] work, Exercise #".
Save trace with a file name in the following format.

> Exercise number-end number-channel letter-wavelength.

For example: a trace made of exercise 81, of channel A from end 1 at 850 nm will have the file label '81-1-A-850'. For example: a trace made of exercise 83, of channel B at 850 nm from end 4 will have the file label '83-4-B-850'.

For example, your eight traces could be labeled:

81-1-A-850	81-1-A-1300
81-1-B-850	81-1-B-1300
81-4-A-850	81-4-A-1300
81-4-B-850	81-4-B-1300

Give the OTDR module to another team. Begin trace analysis of the traces on your computer.

2.7. Maps

The exercises use one of the following maps. All maps use 'S" to indicate a splice.

Map 1

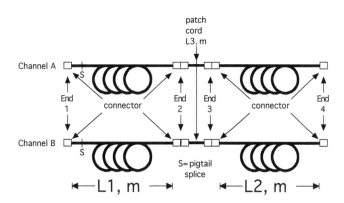

Map 2

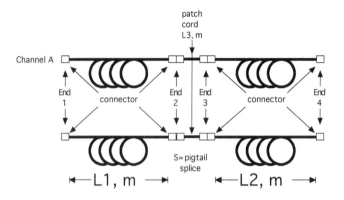

Map 3

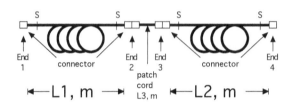

Map 4

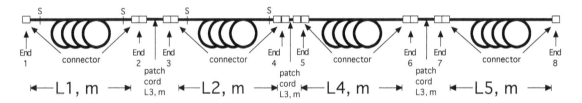

Map 5

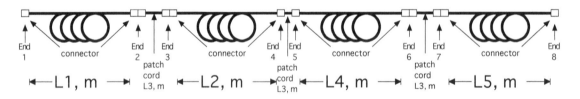

2.8. Fiber Specifications

Wavelength=			850 nm		1300 nm	1300 nm
Fiber=			50μ	62.5μ	50μ	62.5μ
Attenuation rate	dB/km	maximum	3.5	3.5	1.5	1.5
Attenuation rate	dB/km	typical	2.5	2.9	0.7	0.7
NA	----		0.2	0.275	1.479	1.479
IR	----	typical	1.48	1.483	1.479	1.479
Backscatter Coefficient	dB	typical	-68.4	-68	-75.8	-76

Wavelength=			Singlemode 1310 nm	Singlemode 1310 nm	Singlemode 1550 nm	Singlemode 1550 nm
			Singlemode Tight Tube	Loose Tube	Singlemode Tight Tube	Loose Tube
Attenuation rate	dB/km	maximum	1	0.5	1	0.2
Attenuation rate	dB/km	typical	0.4	0.3	0.25	0.2
IR		----	1.4676	1.4676	1.4682	1.4682
Backscatter Coefficient	dB	typical	-77	-77	-82	-82

Connector Loss	For All Fibers At All Wavelengths		
2.5mm, polished	dB/pair	maximum	0.75
2.5mm, polished	dB/pair	typical	0.30
1.25mm, polished	dB/pair	maximum	0.75
1.25mm, polished	dB/pair	typical	0.20
No polish	dB/pair	maximum	0.75
No polish	dB/pair	typical	0.40
Splice Loss	dB/splice	maximum	0.15
Splice Loss	dB/splice	typical	0.10

Troubleshooting Exercise 81

Use Map 2 and 62.5μ specifications.
L1= 100 m to 110 m. L2= 100 m to 110 m. L3= 1 m.

850 Insertion loss Calculations, Method B

Use Maximum Values

Cable length		dB/km				
	X	_		=		dB
# of pairs		dB/pair				
	X	_		=		dB
# splices		dB/splice				
	X			=		dB
			Maximum Insertion Loss=			dB

Use Typical Values

Cable length		dB/km				
_	X	_		=		dB
# of pairs		dB/pair				
_	X	_		=		dB
# splices		dB/splice				
	X			=		dB
			Typical Insertion Loss=			dB

850 nm Acceptance Value Calculation

Maximum	-	Typical			
(	+	)	/2=		dB

850 nm Measured Loss

	Channel A Loss, dB	Channel A Accept/Reject?		Channel B Loss, dB	Channel B Accept/Reject?
Source @ end 1					
Source @ opposite end					

850 nm OTDR Acceptance Value Calculations

OTDR	Maximum		Typical	Acceptance Values	
attenuation rate	(	+	)/2=		dB/km
connector loss	(	+	)/2=		dB/pair
splice loss	(	+	)/2=		dB/splice

1300 Insertion loss Calculations, Method B

Use Maximum Values

Cable length		dB/km				
	X	_		=		dB

# of pairs		dB/pair				
	X	_		=		dB

# splices		dB/splice				
	X			=		dB

Maximum Insertion Loss= [ ] dB

Use Typical Values

Cable length		dB/km				
_	X	_		=		dB

# of pairs		dB/pair				
_	X	_		=		dB

# splices		dB/splice				
	X			=		dB

Typical Insertion Loss= [ ] dB

1300 nm Acceptance Value Calculation

Maximum	-	Typical			
(	+	)	/2=		dB

1300 nm Measured Loss

	Channel A Loss, dB	Channel A Accept/Reject?	Channel B Loss, dB	Channel B Accept/Reject?
Source @ end 1				
Source @ opposite end				

1300 nm OTDR Acceptance Value Calculations

OTDR	Maximum		Typical	Acceptance Values	
attenuation rate	(	+	)/2=		dB/km
connector loss	(	+	)/2=		dB/pair
splice loss	(	+	)/2=		dB/splice

850 nm OTDR Measurements

From end 1					From end 4			
Channel A	OTDR Value	Accept. Value	Acc/ Rej?		**Channel A**	OTDR Value	Accept. Value	Acc/ Rej?
Connector, End 1					Connector, End 4			
Connector, End 2-3					Connector, End 2-3			
Connector, End 4					Connector, End 1			
Fiber length, Seg. 1					Fiber length, Seg. 2			
Fiber length, Seg. 2					Fiber length, Seg. 1			
Attenuation, Seg. 1					Attenuation, Seg. 2			
Attenuation, Seg. 2					Attenuation, Seg. 1			
Channel B					**Channel B**			
Connector, End 1					Connector, End 4			
Connector, End 2-3					Connector, End 2-3			
Connector, End 4					Connector, End 1			
Fiber length, Seg. 1					Fiber length, Seg.2			
Fiber length, Seg.2					Fiber length, Seg.1			
Attenuation, Seg.1					Attenuation, Seg. 2			
Attenuation, Seg.1					Attenuation, Seg. 1			

1300 nm OTDR Measurements

From end 1					From end 4			
Channel A	OTDR Value	Accept. Value	Acc/ Rej?		**Channel A**	OTDR Value	Accept. Value	Acc/ Rej?
Connector, End 1					Connector, End 4			
Connector, End 2-3					Connector, End 2-3			
Connector, End 4					Connector, End 1			
Fiber length, Seg. 1					Fiber length, Seg. 2			
Fiber length, Seg. 2					Fiber length, Seg. 1			
Attenuation, Seg. 1					Attenuation, Seg. 2			
Attenuation, Seg. 2					Attenuation, Seg. 1			
Channel B					**Channel B**			
Connector, End 1					Connector, End 4			
Connector, End 2-3					Connector, End 2-3			
Connector, End 4					Connector, End 1			
Fiber length, Seg. 1					Fiber length, Seg.2			
Fiber length, Seg.2					Fiber length, Seg.1			
Attenuation, Seg.1					Attenuation, Seg. 2			
Attenuation, Seg.1					Attenuation, Seg. 1			

Conclusions: Stress evident? Trace reflects map? All components within acceptance values?

Troubleshooting Exercise 82

Use Map 1 and 62.5μ specifications.
L1= 100 m to 110 m. L2= 100 m to 110 m. L3= 1 m.

850 Insertion loss Calculations, Method B

Use Maximum Values

Cable length		dB/km				
	X	-		=		dB
# of pairs		dB/pair				
	X	-		=		dB
# splices		dB/splice				
	X			=		dB
				Maximum Insertion Loss=		dB

Use Typical Values

Cable length		dB/km				
-	X	-		=		dB
# of pairs		dB/pair				
-	X	-		=		dB
# splices		dB/splice				
	X			=		dB
				Typical Insertion Loss=		dB

850 nm Acceptance Value Calculation

Maximum	-	Typical				
(	+	)	/2=		dB	

850 nm Measured Loss

	Channel A Loss, dB	Channel A Accept/Reject?	Channel B Loss, dB	Channel B Accept/Reject?
Source @ end 1				
Source @ opposite end				

850 nm OTDR Acceptance Value Calculations

OTDR	Maximum		Typical	Acceptance Values	
attenuation rate	(	+	)/2=		dB/km
connector loss	(	+	)/2=		dB/pair
splice loss	(	+	)/2=		dB/splice

1300 Insertion loss Calculations, Method B

Use Maximum Values

Cable length		dB/km				
	X	_		=		dB

# of pairs		dB/pair				
	X	_		=		dB

# splices		dB/splice				
	X			=		dB

Maximum Insertion Loss= [ ] dB

Use Typical Values

Cable length		dB/km			
_	X	_		=	dB

# of pairs		dB/pair			
_	X	_		=	dB

# splices		dB/splice			
	X			=	dB

Typical Insertion Loss= [ ] dB

1300 nm Acceptance Value Calculation

Maximum	-	Typical			
(	+	)	/2=		dB

1300 nm Measured Loss

	Channel A Loss, dB	Channel A Accept/Reject?	Channel B Loss, dB	Channel B Accept/Reject?
Source @ end 1				
Source @ opposite end				

1300 nm OTDR Acceptance Value Calculations

OTDR	Maximum		Typical	Acceptance Values	
attenuation rate	(	+	)/2=		dB/km
connector loss	(	+	)/2=		dB/pair
splice loss	(	+	)/2=		dB/splice

850 nm OTDR Measurements								
From end 1					**From end 4**			
Channel A	OTDR Value	Accept. Value	Acc/ Rej?		**Channel A**	OTDR Value	Accept. Value	Acc/ Rej?
Connector, End 1					Connector, End 4			
Connector, End 2-3					Connector, End 2-3			
Connector, End 4					Connector, End 1			
Fiber length, Seg. 1					Fiber length, Seg. 2			
Fiber length, Seg. 2					Fiber length, Seg. 1			
Attenuation, Seg. 1					Attenuation, Seg. 2			
Attenuation, Seg. 2					Attenuation, Seg. 1			
Channel B					**Channel B**			
Connector, End 1					Connector, End 4			
Connector, End 2-3					Connector, End 2-3			
Connector, End 4					Connector, End 1			
Fiber length, Seg. 1					Fiber length, Seg.2			
Fiber length, Seg.2					Fiber length, Seg.1			
Attenuation, Seg.1					Attenuation, Seg. 2			
Attenuation, Seg.1					Attenuation, Seg. 1			

1300 nm OTDR Measurements								
From end 1					**From end 4**			
Channel A	OTDR Value	Accept. Value	Acc/ Rej?		**Channel A**	OTDR Value	Accept. Value	Acc/ Rej?
Connector, End 1					Connector, End 4			
Connector, End 2-3					Connector, End 2-3			
Connector, End 4					Connector, End 1			
Fiber length, Seg. 1					Fiber length, Seg. 2			
Fiber length, Seg. 2					Fiber length, Seg. 1			
Attenuation, Seg. 1					Attenuation, Seg. 2			
Attenuation, Seg. 2					Attenuation, Seg. 1			
Channel B					**Channel B**			
Connector, End 1					Connector, End 4			
Connector, End 2-3					Connector, End 2-3			
Connector, End 4					Connector, End 1			
Fiber length, Seg. 1					Fiber length, Seg.2			
Fiber length, Seg.2					Fiber length, Seg.1			
Attenuation, Seg.1					Attenuation, Seg. 2			
Attenuation, Seg.1					Attenuation, Seg. 1			

Conclusions: Stress evident? Trace reflects map? All components within acceptance values?

Troubleshooting Exercise 83

Use Map 4 and 62.5μ specifications.
L1= 100 m. L2= 100 m. L3= 1 m. L4= 100 m. L5= 100 m.

850 Insertion loss Calculations, Method B

Use Maximum Values

Cable length		dB/km				
	X	-		=		dB
# of pairs		dB/pair				
	X	-		=		dB
# splices		dB/splice				
	X			=		dB
				Maximum Insertion Loss=		dB

Use Typical Values

Cable length		dB/km				
-	X	-		=		dB
# of pairs		dB/pair				
-	X	-		=		dB
# splices		dB/splice				
	X			=		dB
				Typical Insertion Loss=		dB

850 nm Acceptance Value Calculation

Maximum		Typical				
(	+	)	/2=		dB

850 nm Measured Loss

	Loss, dB	Accept/Reject?
Source @ end 1		
Source @ opposite end		

850 nm OTDR Acceptance Value Calculations

OTDR	Maximum	Typical	Acceptance Values	
attenuation rate	(	+	)/2=	dB/km
connector loss	(	+	)/2=	dB/pair
splice loss	(	+	)/2=	dB/splice

1300 Insertion loss Calculations, Method B

Use Maximum Values

Cable length		dB/km				
	X	_		=		dB

# of pairs		dB/pair				
	X	_		=		dB

# splices		dB/splice				
	X			=		dB

Maximum Insertion Loss= [ ] dB

Use Typical Values

Cable length		dB/km				
_	X	_		=		dB

# of pairs		dB/pair				
_	X	_		=		dB

# splices		dB/splice				
	X			=		dB

Typical Insertion Loss= [ ] dB

1300 nm Acceptance Value Calculation

Maximum	-	Typical			
(	+	)	/2=		dB

1300 nm Measured Loss

	Loss, dB	Accept/Reject?
Source @ end 1		
Source @ opposite end		

1300 nm OTDR Acceptance Value Calculations

OTDR	Maximum	Typical	Acceptance Values	
attenuation rate	(	+	)/2=	dB/km
connector loss	(	+	)/2=	dB/pair
splice loss	(	+	)/2=	dB/splice

850 nm OTDR Measurements							
From end 1				**From end 8**			
Channel A	OTDR Value	Accept. Value	Acc/ Rej?	**Channel A**	OTDR Value	Accept. Value	Acc/ Rej?
Connector, End 1				Connector, End 8			
Connector, End 2-3				Connector, End 6-7			
Connector, End 4-5				Connector, End 4-5			
Connector, End 6-7				Connector, End 2-3			
Connector, End 8				Connector, End 1			
Fiber length, Seg. 1				Fiber length, Seg. 4			
Fiber length, Seg. 2				Fiber length, Seg. 3			
Fiber length, Seg. 3				Fiber length, Seg. 2			
Fiber length, Seg. 4				Fiber length, Seg. 1			
Attenuation, Seg. 1				Attenuation, Seg. 4			
Attenuation, Seg. 2				Attenuation, Seg. 3			
Attenuation, Seg. 3				Attenuation, Seg. 2			
Attenuation, Seg. 4				Attenuation, Seg. 1			

1300 nm OTDR Measurements							
From end 1				**From end 8**			
Channel A	OTDR Value	Accept. Value	Acc/ Rej?	**Channel A**	OTDR Value	Accept. Value	Acc/ Rej?
Connector, End 1				Connector, End 8			
Connector, End 2-3				Connector, End 6-7			
Connector, End 4-5				Connector, End 4-5			
Connector, End 6-7				Connector, End 2-3			
Connector, End 8				Connector, End 1			
Fiber length, Seg. 1				Fiber length, Seg. 4			
Fiber length, Seg. 2				Fiber length, Seg. 3			
Fiber length, Seg. 3				Fiber length, Seg. 2			
Fiber length, Seg. 4				Fiber length, Seg. 1			
Attenuation, Seg. 1				Attenuation, Seg. 4			
Attenuation, Seg. 2				Attenuation, Seg. 3			
Attenuation, Seg. 3				Attenuation Seg. 2			
Attenuation, Seg. 4				Attenuation, Seg. 1			

Conclusions: Stress evident? Trace reflects map? All components within acceptance values?

Troubleshooting Exercise 84

Use Map 5 and 62.5μ specifications.
L1= 100 m. L2= 100 m. L3= 1 m. L4= 100 m. L5= 100 m.

850 Insertion loss Calculations, Method B

Use Maximum Values

Cable length		dB/km				
	X	_		=		dB

# of pairs		dB/pair				
	X	_		=		dB

# splices		dB/splice				
	X			=		dB

Maximum Insertion Loss= ___ dB

Use Typical Values

Cable length		dB/km				
_	X	_		=		dB

# of pairs		dB/pair				
_	X	_		=		dB

# splices		dB/splice				
	X			=		dB

Typical Insertion Loss= ___ dB

850 nm Acceptance Value Calculation

Maximum	-	Typical			
(	+	)	/2=		dB

850 nm Measured Loss

	Loss, dB	Accept/Reject?
Source @ end 1		
Source @ opposite end		

850 nm OTDR Acceptance Value Calculations

OTDR	Maximum		Typical	Acceptance Values	
attenuation rate	(	+	)/2=		dB/km
connector loss	(	+	)/2=		dB/pair
splice loss	(	+	)/2=		dB/splice

1300 Insertion loss Calculations, Method B

Use Maximum Values

Cable length		dB/km				
	X	_		=		dB

# of pairs		dB/pair				
	X	_		=		dB

# splices		dB/splice				
	X			=		dB
			Maximum Insertion Loss=			dB

Use Typical Values

Cable length		dB/km				
_	X	_		=		dB

# of pairs		dB/pair				
_	X	_		=		dB

# splices		dB/splice				
	X			=		dB
			Typical Insertion Loss=			dB

1300 nm Acceptance Value Calculation

Maximum	-	Typical				
(	+	)	/2=		dB	

1300 nm Measured Loss

	Loss, dB	Accept/Reject?
Source @ end 1		
Source @ opposite end		

1300 nm OTDR Acceptance Value Calculations

OTDR	Maximum		Typical	Acceptance Values	
attenuation rate	(	+	)/2=		dB/km
connector loss	(	+	)/2=		dB/pair
splice loss	(	+	)/2=		dB/splice

850 nm OTDR Measurements								
From end 1					**From end 8**			
Channel A	OTDR Value	Accept. Value	Acc/ Rej?		**Channel A**	OTDR Value	Accept. Value	Acc/ Rej?
Connector, End 1					Connector, End 8			
Connector, End 2-3					Connector, End 6-7			
Connector, End 4-5					Connector, End 4-5			
Connector, End 6-7					Connector, End 2-3			
Connector, End 8					Connector, End 1			
Fiber length, Seg. 1					Fiber length, Seg. 4			
Fiber length, Seg. 2					Fiber length, Seg. 3			
Fiber length, Seg. 3					Fiber length, Seg. 2			
Fiber length, Seg. 4					Fiber length, Seg. 1			
Attenuation, Seg. 1					Attenuation, Seg. 4			
Attenuation, Seg. 2					Attenuation, Seg. 3			
Attenuation, Seg. 3					Attenuation, Seg. 2			
Attenuation, Seg. 4					Attenuation, Seg. 1			

1300 nm OTDR Measurements								
From end 1					**From end 8**			
Channel A	OTDR Value	Accept. Value	Acc/ Rej?		**Channel A**	OTDR Value	Accept. Value	Acc/ Rej?
Connector, End 1					Connector, End 8			
Connector, End 2-3					Connector, End 6-7			
Connector, End 4-5					Connector, End 4-5			
Connector, End 6-7					Connector, End 2-3			
Connector, End 8					Connector, End 1			
Fiber length, Seg. 1					Fiber length, Seg. 4			
Fiber length, Seg. 2					Fiber length, Seg. 3			
Fiber length, Seg. 3					Fiber length, Seg. 2			
Fiber length, Seg. 4					Fiber length, Seg. 1			
Attenuation, Seg. 1					Attenuation, Seg. 4			
Attenuation, Seg. 2					Attenuation, Seg. 3			
Attenuation, Seg. 3					Attenuation, Seg. 2			
Attenuation, Seg. 4					Attenuation, Seg. 1			

Conclusions: Stress evident? Trace reflects map? All components within acceptance values?

Troubleshooting Exercise 85

Use Map 3 and 50μ specifications.
L1= 206 m. L2= 306 m. L3= 2 m.

850 Insertion loss Calculations, Method B

Use Maximum Values

Cable length		dB/km				
	X	_		=		dB
# of pairs		dB/pair				
	X	_		=		dB
# splices		dB/splice				
	X			=		dB
				Maximum Insertion Loss=		dB

Use Typical Values

Cable length		dB/km				
_	X	_		=		dB
# of pairs		dB/pair				
_	X	_		=		dB
# splices		dB/splice				
	X			=		dB
				Typical Insertion Loss=		dB

850 nm Acceptance Value Calculation

Maximum	-	Typical				
(	+	)	/2=			dB

1300 nm Measured Loss

	Loss, dB	Accept/Reject?
Source @ end 1		
Source @ opposite end		

850 nm OTDR Acceptance Value Calculations

OTDR	Maximum		Typical	Acceptance Values	
attenuation rate	(	+	)/2=		dB/km
connector loss	(	+	)/2=		dB/pair
splice loss	(	+	)/2=		dB/splice

1300 Insertion loss Calculations, Method B

Use Maximum Values

Cable length		dB/km				
	X	-		=		dB

# of pairs		dB/pair				
	X	-		=		dB

# splices		dB/splice				
	X			=		dB

Maximum Insertion Loss= [ ] dB

Use Typical Values

Cable length		dB/km				
-	X	-		=		dB

# of pairs		dB/pair				
-	X	-		=		dB

# splices		dB/splice				
	X			=		dB

Typical Insertion Loss= [ ] dB

1300 nm Acceptance Value Calculation

Maximum	-		Typical			
(	+		)	/2=		dB

1300 nm Measured Loss

	Loss, dB	Accept/Reject?
Source @ end 1		
Source @ opposite end		

1300 nm OTDR Acceptance Value Calculations

OTDR	Maximum		Typical	Acceptance Values	
attenuation rate	(	+	)/2=		dB/km
connector loss	(	+	)/2=		dB/pair
splice loss	(	+	)/2=		dB/splice

850 nm OTDR Measurements								
From end 1					**From end 4**			
Channel A	OTDR Value	Accept. Value	Acc/ Rej?		**Channel A**	OTDR Value	Accept. Value	Acc/ Rej?
Connector, End 1					Connector, End 4			
Connector, End 2-3					Connector, End 2-3			
Connector, End 4					Connector, End 1			
Fiber length, Seg. 1					Fiber length, Seg. 2			
Fiber length, Seg. 2					Fiber length, Seg. 1			
Attenuation, Seg. 1					Attenuation, Seg. 2			
Attenuation, Seg. 2					Attenuation, Seg. 1			

1300 nm OTDR Measurements								
From end 1					**From end 4**			
Channel A	OTDR Value	Accept. Value	Acc/ Rej?		**Channel A**	OTDR Value	Accept. Value	Acc/ Rej?
Connector, End 1					Connector, End 4			
Connector, End 2-3					Connector, End 2-3			
Connector, End 4					Connector, End 1			
Fiber length, Seg. 1					Fiber length, Seg. 2			
Fiber length, Seg. 2					Fiber length, Seg. 1			
Attenuation, Seg. 1					Attenuation, Seg. 2			
Attenuation, Seg. 2					Attenuation, Seg. 1			

Conclusions: Stress evident? Trace reflects map? All components within acceptance values?

Troubleshooting Exercise 86

Use Map 3 and 50μ specifications.
L1= 306 m. L2= 206 m. L3= 2 m.

850 Insertion loss Calculations, Method B

Use Maximum Values

Cable length		dB/km				
	X	-		=		dB

# of pairs		dB/pair				
	X	-		=		dB

# splices		dB/splice				
	X			=		dB

Maximum Insertion Loss= [ ] dB

Use Typical Values

Cable length		dB/km				
-	X	-		=		dB

# of pairs		dB/pair				
-	X	-		=		dB

# splices		dB/splice				
	X			=		dB

Typical Insertion Loss= [ ] dB

850 nm Acceptance Value Calculation

Maximum	-	Typical				
(	+	)	/2=		dB	

850 nm Measured Loss

	Loss, dB	Accept/Reject?
Source @ end 1		
Source @ opposite end		

850 nm OTDR Acceptance Value Calculations

OTDR	Maximum		Typical	Acceptance Values	
attenuation rate	(	+	)/2=		dB/km
connector loss	(	+	)/2=		dB/pair
splice loss	(	+	)/2=		dB/splice

1300 Insertion loss Calculations, Method B

Use Maximum Values

Cable length		dB/km				
	X	_		=		dB

# of pairs		dB/pair				
	X	_		=		dB

# splices		dB/splice				
	X			=		dB
				Maximum Insertion Loss=		dB

Use Typical Values

Cable length		dB/km				
_	X	_		=		dB

# of pairs		dB/pair				
_	X	_		=		dB

# splices		dB/splice				
	X			=		dB
				Typical Insertion Loss=		dB

1300 nm Acceptance Value Calculation

Maximum	-	Typical				
(	+	)	/2=		dB	

1300 nm Measured Loss

	Loss, dB	Accept/Reject?
Source @ end 1		
Source @ opposite end		

1300 nm OTDR Acceptance Value Calculations

OTDR		Maximum		Typical	Acceptance Values	
attenuation rate		(	+	)/2=		dB/km
connector loss		(	+	)/2=		dB/pair
splice loss		(	+	)/2=		dB/splice

850 nm OTDR Measurements								
From end 1					**From end 4**			
Channel A	OTDR Value	Accept. Value	Acc/ Rej?		**Channel A**	OTDR Value	Accept. Value	Acc/ Rej?
Connector, End 1					Connector, End 4			
Connector, End 2-3					Connector, End 2-3			
Connector, End 4					Connector, End 1			
Fiber length, Seg. 1					Fiber length, Seg. 2			
Fiber length, Seg. 2					Fiber length, Seg. 1			
Attenuation, Seg. 1					Attenuation, Seg. 2			
Attenuation, Seg. 2					Attenuation, Seg. 1			

1300 nm OTDR Measurements								
From end 1					**From end 4**			
Channel A	OTDR Value	Accept. Value	Acc/ Rej?		**Channel A**	OTDR Value	Accept. Value	Acc/ Rej?
Connector, End 1					Connector, End 4			
Connector, End 2-3					Connector, End 2-3			
Connector, End 4					Connector, End 1			
Fiber length, Seg. 1					Fiber length, Seg. 2			
Fiber length, Seg. 2					Fiber length, Seg. 1			
Attenuation, Seg. 1					Attenuation, Seg. 2			
Attenuation, Seg. 2					Attenuation, Seg. 1			

Conclusions: Stress evident? Trace reflects map? All components within acceptance values?

Troubleshooting Exercise 87

Use Map 3 and singlemode specifications.
L1= 206 m. L2= 306 m. L3= 2 m.

1310 Insertion loss Calculations, Method B

Use Maximum Values

Cable length		dB/km				
	X	-		=		dB

# of pairs		dB/pair				
	X	-		=		dB

# splices		dB/splice				
	X			=		dB

Maximum Insertion Loss= _____ dB

Use Typical Values

Cable length		dB/km				
-	X	-		=		dB

# of pairs		dB/pair				
-	X	-		=		dB

# splices		dB/splice				
	X			=		dB

Typical Insertion Loss= _____ dB

1310 nm Acceptance Value Calculation

Maximum	-	Typical			
(	+	)	/2=		dB

1310 nm Measured Loss

	Loss, dB	Accept/Reject?
Source @ end 1		
Source @ opposite end		

1310 nm OTDR Acceptance Value Calculations

OTDR	Maximum	Typical	Acceptance Values	
attenuation rate	(	+	)/2=	dB/km
connector loss	(	+	)/2=	dB/pair
splice loss	(	+	)/2=	dB/splice

1550 Insertion loss Calculations, Method B

Use Maximum Values

Cable length		dB/km				
	X	-		=		dB
# of pairs		dB/pair				
	X	-		=		dB
# splices		dB/splice				
	X			=		dB
				Maximum Insertion Loss=		dB

Use Typical Values

Cable length		dB/km				
-	X	-		=		dB
# of pairs		dB/pair				
-	X	-		=		dB
# splices		dB/splice				
	X			=		dB
				Typical Insertion Loss=		dB

1550 nm Acceptance Value Calculation

Maximum	-	Typical			
(	+	)	/2=		dB

1550 nm Measured Loss

	Loss, dB	Accept/Reject?
Source @ end 1		
Source @ opposite end		

1550 nm OTDR Acceptance Value Calculations

OTDR	Maximum	Typical	Acceptance Values	
attenuation rate	(	+	)/2=	dB/km
connector loss	(	+	)/2=	dB/pair
splice loss	(	+	)/2=	dB/splice

1310 nm OTDR Measurements								
From end 1				**From end 4**				
Channel A	OTDR Value	Accept. Value	Acc/ Rej?	**Channel A**	OTDR Value	Accept. Value	Acc/ Rej?
Connector, End 1				Connector, End 4			
Connector, End 2-3				Connector, End 2-3			
Connector, End 4				Connector, End 1			
Fiber length, Seg. 1				Fiber length, Seg. 2			
Fiber length, Seg. 2				Fiber length, Seg. 1			
Attenuation, Seg. 1				Attenuation, Seg. 2			
Attenuation, Seg. 2				Attenuation, Seg. 1			

1550 nm OTDR Measurements								
From end 1				**From end 4**				
Channel A	OTDR Value	Accept. Value	Acc/ Rej?	**Channel A**	OTDR Value	Accept. Value	Acc/ Rej?
Connector, End 1				Connector, End 4			
Connector, End 2-3				Connector, End 2-3			
Connector, End 4				Connector, End 1			
Fiber length, Seg. 1				Fiber length, Seg. 2			
Fiber length, Seg. 2				Fiber length, Seg. 1			
Attenuation, Seg. 1				Attenuation, Seg. 2			
Attenuation, Seg. 2				Attenuation, Seg. 1			

Conclusions: Stress evident? Trace reflects map? All components within acceptance values?

Troubleshooting Exercise 88

Use Map 3 and singlemode specifications.
L1= 206 m. L2= 306 m. L3= 2 m.

1310 Insertion loss Calculations, Method B

Use Maximum Values

Cable length		dB/km				
	X	_		=		dB
# of pairs		dB/pair				
	X	_		=		dB
# splices		dB/splice				
	X			=		dB
			Maximum Insertion Loss=			dB

Use Typical Values

Cable length		dB/km			
_	X	_		=	dB
# of pairs		dB/pair			
_	X	_		=	dB
# splices		dB/splice			
	X			=	dB
			Typical Insertion Loss=		dB

1310 nm Acceptance Value Calculation

Maximum	-	Typical			
(	+	)	/2=		dB

1310 nm Measured Loss

		Loss, dB	Accept/Reject?
Source @ end 1			
Source @ opposite end			

1310 nm OTDR Acceptance Value Calculations

OTDR	Maximum		Typical	Acceptance Values	
attenuation rate	(	+	)/2=		dB/km
connector loss	(	+	)/2=		dB/pair
splice loss	(	+	)/2=		dB/splice

1550 Insertion loss Calculations, Method B

Use Maximum Values

Cable length		dB/km				
	X	_		=		dB

# of pairs		dB/pair				
	X	_		=		dB

# splices		dB/splice				
	X			=		dB

Maximum Insertion Loss= [ ] dB

Use Typical Values

Cable length		dB/km				
_	X	_		=		dB

# of pairs		dB/pair				
_	X	_		=		dB

# splices		dB/splice				
	X			=		dB

Typical Insertion Loss= [ ] dB

1550 nm Acceptance Value Calculation

Maximum	-	Typical			
(	+	)	/2=		dB

1550 nm Measured Loss

	Loss, dB	Accept/Reject?
Source @ end 1		
Source @ opposite end		

1550 nm OTDR Acceptance Value Calculations

OTDR	Maximum		Typical	Acceptance Values	
attenuation rate	(	+	)/2=		dB/km
connector loss	(	+	)/2=		dB/pair
splice loss	(	+	)/2=		dB/splice

1310 nm OTDR Measurements									
From end 1					**From end 4**				
Channel A	OTDR Value	Accept. Value	Acc/ Rej?		**Channel A**	OTDR Value	Accept. Value	Acc/ Rej?
Connector, End 1					Connector, End 4			
Connector, End 2-3					Connector, End 2-3			
Connector, End 4					Connector, End 1			
Fiber length, Seg. 1					Fiber length, Seg. 2			
Fiber length, Seg. 2					Fiber length, Seg. 1			
Attenuation, Seg. 1					Attenuation, Seg. 2			
Attenuation, Seg. 2					Attenuation, Seg. 1			

1550 nm OTDR Measurements									
From end 1					**From end 4**				
Channel A	OTDR Value	Accept. Value	Acc/ Rej?		**Channel A**	OTDR Value	Accept. Value	Acc/ Rej?
Connector, End 1					Connector, End 4			
Connector, End 2-3					Connector, End 2-3			
Connector, End 4					Connector, End 1			
Fiber length, Seg. 1					Fiber length, Seg. 2			
Fiber length, Seg. 2					Fiber length, Seg. 1			
Attenuation, Seg. 1					Attenuation, Seg. 2			
Attenuation, Seg. 2					Attenuation, Seg. 1			

Conclusions: Stress evident? Trace reflects map? All components within acceptance values?

Troubleshooting Exercise 89

Use Map 3 and singlemode specifications.
L1= 302 m. L2= 402 m. L3= 2 m.

1310 Insertion loss Calculations, Method B

Use Maximum Values

Cable length		dB/km				
	X	_		=		dB

# of pairs		dB/pair				
	X	_		=		dB

# splices		dB/splice				
	X			=		dB

Maximum Insertion Loss= dB

Use Typical Values

Cable length		dB/km			
_	X	_		=	dB

# of pairs		dB/pair			
_	X	_		=	dB

# splices		dB/splice			
	X			=	dB

Typical Insertion Loss= dB

1310 nm Acceptance Value Calculation

Maximum	-	Typical			
(	+	)	/2=		dB

1310 nm Measured Loss

	Loss, dB	Accept/Reject?
Source @ end 1		
Source @ opposite end		

1310 nm OTDR Acceptance Value Calculations

OTDR	Maximum		Typical	Acceptance Values	
attenuation rate	(	+	)/2=		dB/km
connector loss	(	+	)/2=		dB/pair
splice loss	(	+	)/2=		dB/splice

1550 Insertion loss Calculations, Method B

Use Maximum Values

Cable length		dB/km				
	X	_		=		dB

# of pairs		dB/pair				
	X	_		=		dB

# splices		dB/splice				
	X			=		dB

Maximum Insertion Loss= [ ] dB

Use Typical Values

Cable length		dB/km				
_	X	_		=		dB

# of pairs		dB/pair				
_	X	_		=		dB

# splices		dB/splice				
	X			=		dB

Typical Insertion Loss= [ ] dB

1550 nm Acceptance Value Calculation

Maximum	-	Typical			
(	+	)	/2=		dB

1550 nm Measured Loss

	Loss, dB	Accept/Reject?
Source @ end 1		
Source @ opposite end		

1550 nm OTDR Acceptance Value Calculations

OTDR	Maximum		Typical	Acceptance Values	
attenuation rate	(	+	)/2=		dB/km
connector loss	(	+	)/2=		dB/pair
splice loss	(	+	)/2=		dB/splice

1310 nm OTDR Measurements								
From end 1				**From end 4**				
Channel A	OTDR Value	Accept. Value	Acc/ Rej?	**Channel A**	OTDR Value	Accept. Value	Acc/ Rej?	
Connector, End 1				Connector, End 4				
Connector, End 2-3				Connector, End 2-3				
Connector, End 4				Connector, End 1				
Fiber length, Seg. 1				Fiber length, Seg. 2				
Fiber length, Seg. 2				Fiber length, Seg. 1				
Attenuation, Seg. 1				Attenuation, Seg. 2				
Attenuation, Seg. 2				Attenuation, Seg. 1				

1550 nm OTDR Measurements								
From end 1				**From end 4**				
Channel A	OTDR Value	Accept. Value	Acc/ Rej?	**Channel A**	OTDR Value	Accept. Value	Acc/ Rej?	
Connector, End 1				Connector, End 4				
Connector, End 2-3				Connector, End 2-3				
Connector, End 4				Connector, End 1				
Fiber length, Seg. 1				Fiber length, Seg. 2				
Fiber length, Seg. 2				Fiber length, Seg. 1				
Attenuation, Seg. 1				Attenuation, Seg. 2				
Attenuation, Seg. 2				Attenuation, Seg. 1				

Conclusions: Stress evident? Trace reflects map? All components within acceptance values?

Troubleshooting Exercise 90

Use Map 3 and singlemode specifications.
L1= 502 m. L2= 302 m. L3= 2 m.

1310 Insertion loss Calculations, Method B

Use Maximum Values

Cable length		dB/km				
	X	-		=		dB

# of pairs		dB/pair				
	X	-		=		dB

# splices		dB/splice				
	X			=		dB

Maximum Insertion Loss= ___ dB

Use Typical Values

Cable length		dB/km				
-	X	-		=		dB

# of pairs		dB/pair				
-	X	-		=		dB

# splices		dB/splice				
	X			=		dB

Typical Insertion Loss= ___ dB

1310 nm Acceptance Value Calculation

Maximum	-	Typical			
(	+	)	/2=		dB

1310 nm Measured Loss

	Loss, dB	Accept/Reject?
Source @ end 1		
Source @ opposite end		

1310 nm OTDR Acceptance Value Calculations

OTDR	Maximum		Typical	Acceptance Values	
attenuation rate	(	+	)/2=		dB/km
connector loss	(	+	)/2=		dB/pair
splice loss	(	+	)/2=		dB/splice

1550 Insertion loss Calculations, Method B

Use Maximum Values

Cable length		dB/km			
	X	_	=		dB

# of pairs		dB/pair			
	X	_	=		dB

# splices		dB/splice			
	X		=		dB
			Maximum Insertion Loss=		dB

Use Typical Values

Cable length		dB/km			
_	X	_	=		dB

# of pairs		dB/pair			
_	X	_	=		dB

# splices		dB/splice			
	X		=		dB
			Typical Insertion Loss=		dB

1550 nm Acceptance Value Calculation

Maximum	-	Typical			
(	+	)	/2=		dB

1550 nm Measured Loss

	Loss, dB	Accept/Reject?
Source @ end 1		
Source @ opposite end		

1550 nm OTDR Acceptance Value Calculations

OTDR	Maximum		Typical	Acceptance Values	
attenuation rate	(	+	)/2=		dB/km
connector loss	(	+	)/2=		dB/pair
splice loss	(	+	)/2=		dB/splice

1310 nm OTDR Measurements								
From end 1					**From end 4**			
Channel A	OTDR Value	Accept. Value	Acc/ Rej?		**Channel A**	OTDR Value	Accept. Value	Acc/ Rej?
Connector, End 1					Connector, End 4			
Connector, End 2-3					Connector, End 2-3			
Connector, End 4					Connector, End 1			
Fiber length, Seg. 1					Fiber length, Seg. 2			
Fiber length, Seg. 2					Fiber length, Seg. 1			
Attenuation, Seg. 1					Attenuation, Seg. 2			
Attenuation, Seg. 2					Attenuation, Seg. 1			

1550 nm OTDR Measurements								
From end 1					**From end 4**			
Channel A	OTDR Value	Accept. Value	Acc/ Rej?		**Channel A**	OTDR Value	Accept. Value	Acc/ Rej?
Connector, End 1					Connector, End 4			
Connector, End 2-3					Connector, End 2-3			
Connector, End 4					Connector, End 1			
Fiber length, Seg. 1					Fiber length, Seg. 2			
Fiber length, Seg. 2					Fiber length, Seg. 1			
Attenuation, Seg. 1					Attenuation, Seg. 2			
Attenuation, Seg. 2					Attenuation, Seg. 1			

Conclusions: Stress evident? Trace reflects map? All components within acceptance values?

3. Instructions For Trace Interpretation Exercises

The following pages contain traces of troubleshooting laboratories. The traces are 62.5μ, 850 nm traces.

Review each trace and answer these questions:

1] Are the cursers properly placed?

2] If one or more curser is improperly placed, which curser(s) is improperly placed?

3] If one or more curser is improperly placed, what placement rule is violated?

4] If the cursers are properly placed, what is being measured?

5] Using standard 62.5μ acceptance values, is the measured value acceptable?

Traces, Labs 61-63
Traces, Channel A, End 1

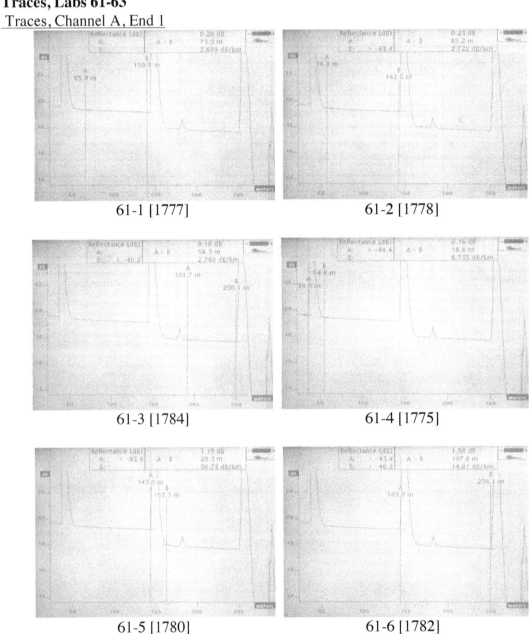

61-1 [1777]	61-2 [1778]
61-3 [1784]	61-4 [1775]
61-5 [1780]	61-6 [1782]

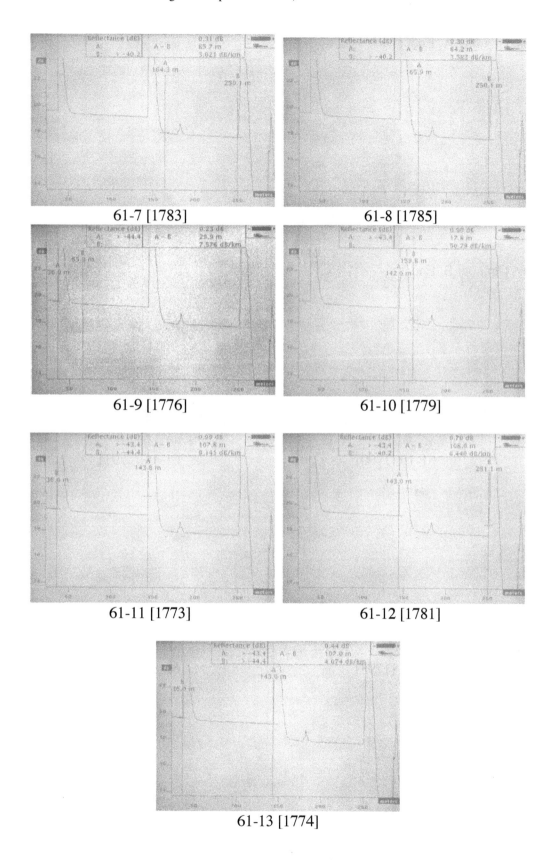

61-7 [1783]

61-8 [1785]

61-9 [1776]

61-10 [1779]

61-11 [1773]

61-12 [1781]

61-13 [1774]

Traces, Channel A, End 4

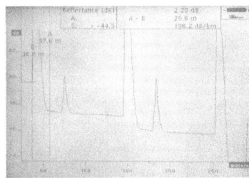

61-14 [1786]

Traces, Channel B, End 1

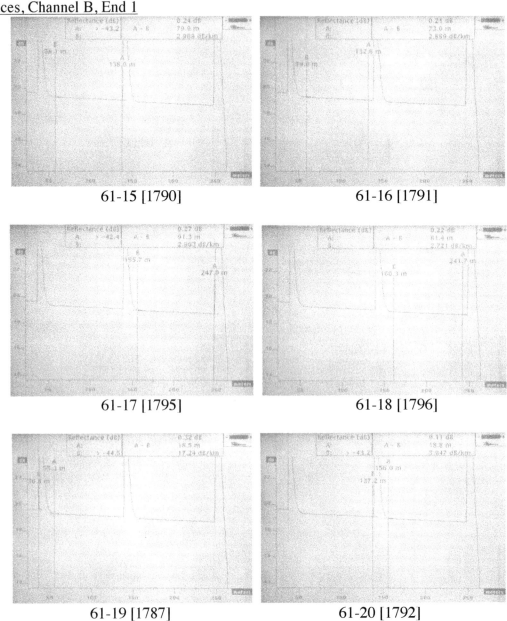

61-15 [1790]   61-16 [1791]

61-17 [1795]   61-18 [1796]

61-19 [1787]   61-20 [1792]

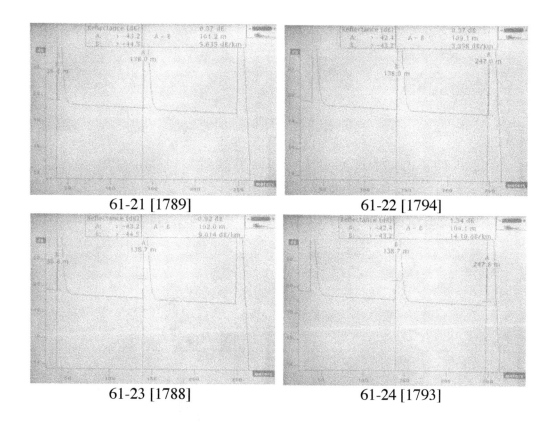

61-21 [1789] 61-22 [1794]

61-23 [1788] 61-24 [1793]

Traces, Channel B, End 4

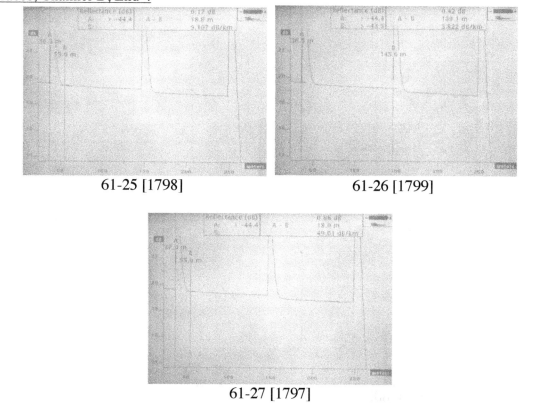

61-25 [1798] 61-26 [1799]

61-27 [1797]

Traces, End 1

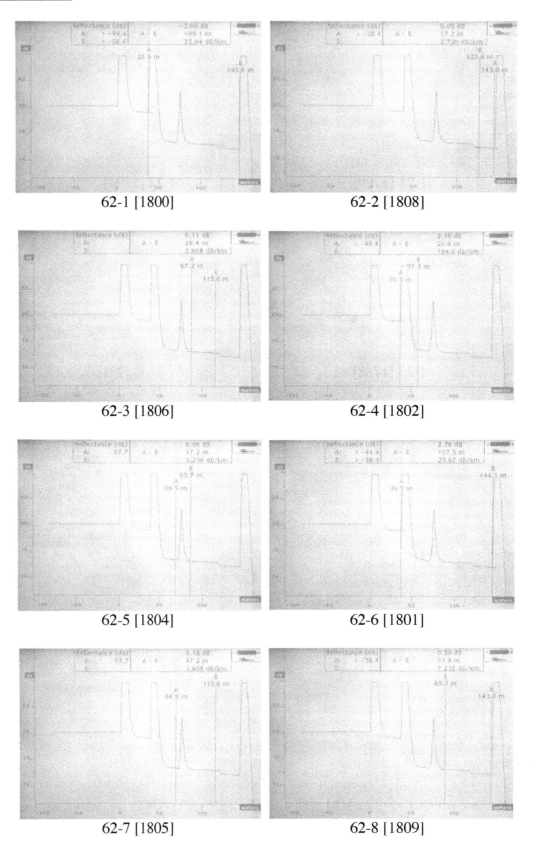

62-1 [1800]   62-2 [1808]

62-3 [1806]   62-4 [1802]

62-5 [1804]   62-6 [1801]

62-7 [1805]   62-8 [1809]

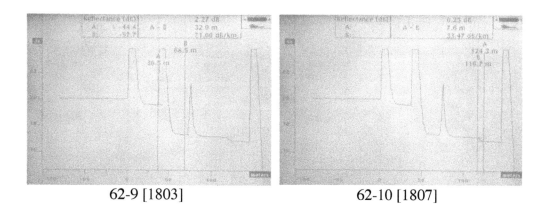

62-9 [1803]   62-10 [1807]

Traces, End 2

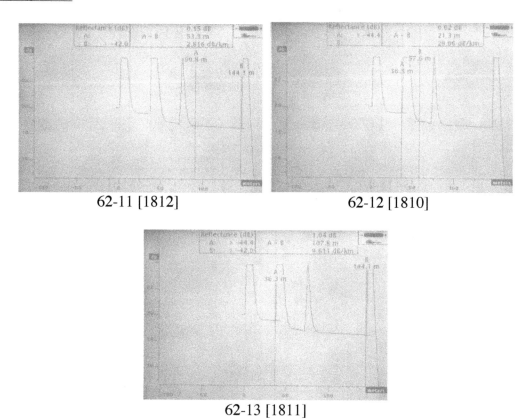

62-11 [1812]   62-12 [1810]

62-13 [1811]

Traces, Channel A, End 1

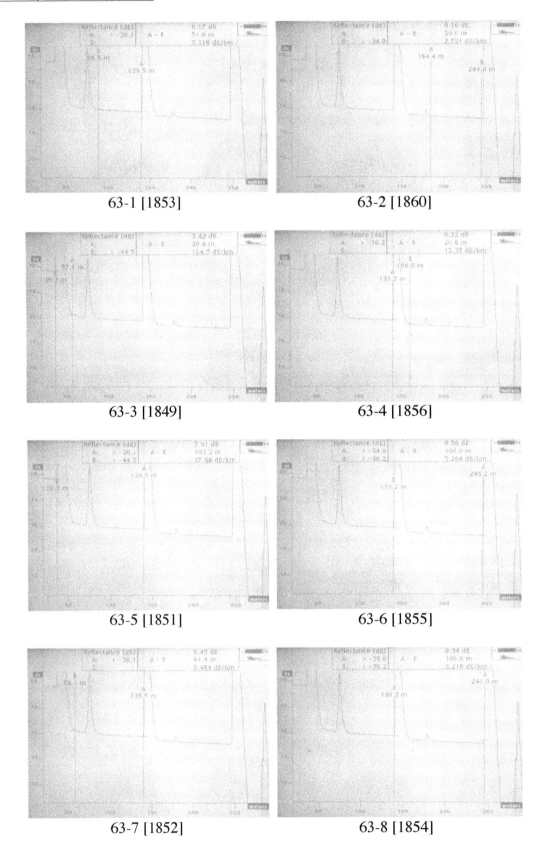

63-1 [1853]

63-2 [1860]

63-3 [1849]

63-4 [1856]

63-5 [1851]

63-6 [1855]

63-7 [1852]

63-8 [1854]

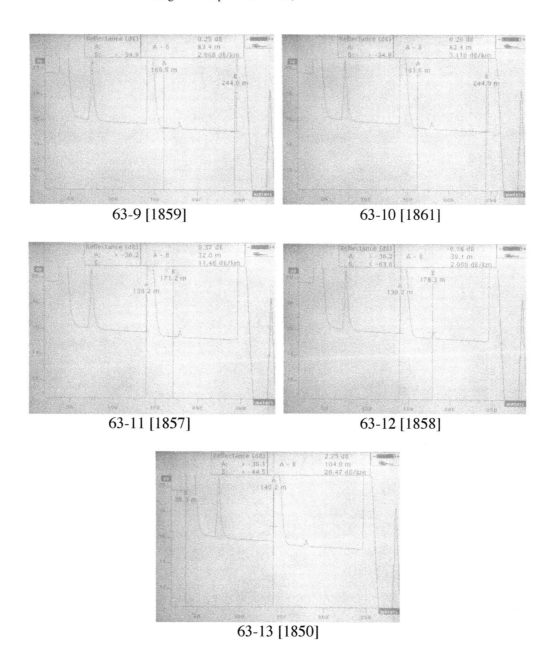

63-9 [1859]   63-10 [1861]

63-11 [1857]   63-12 [1858]

63-13 [1850]

Traces, Channel A, End 4

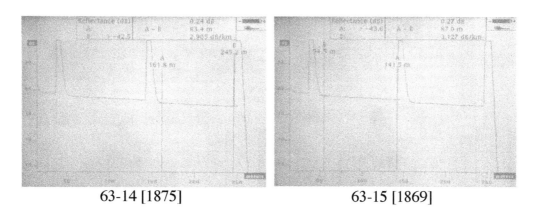

63-14 [1875]   63-15 [1869]

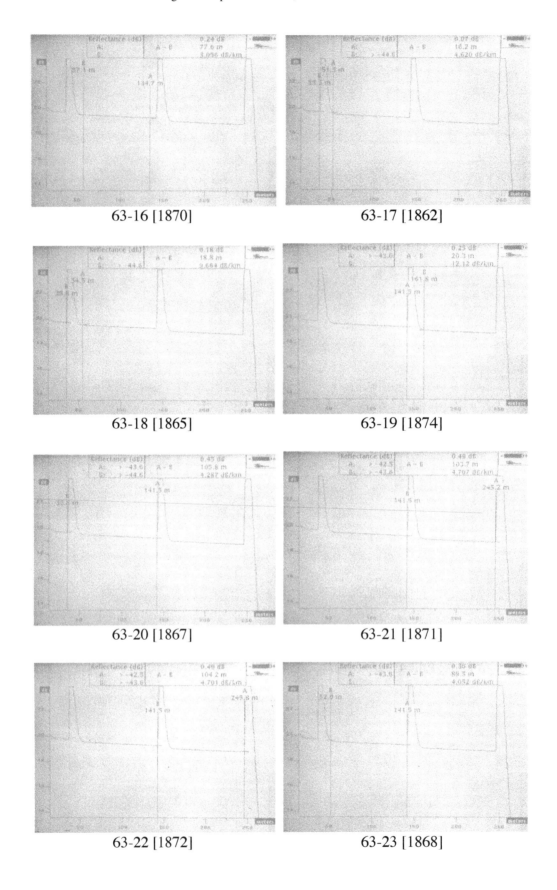

63-16 [1870]

63-17 [1862]

63-18 [1865]

63-19 [1874]

63-20 [1867]

63-21 [1871]

63-22 [1872]

63-23 [1868]

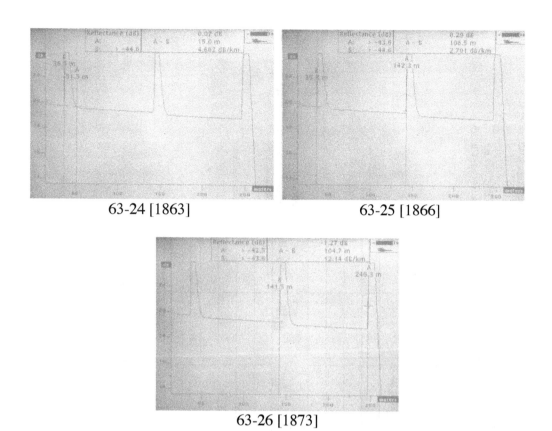

63-24 [1863]   63-25 [1866]

63-26 [1873]

Method Style/Type	Connector Color	INITIAL APPEARANCE		REWORK APPEARANCE		METHOD B INITIAL TEST SOURCE@A SOURCE @B	METHOD B TEST> REWORK SOURCE@A SOURCE @B	NOTES Appearance: G or NG per Ch. 20
		A	B	A	B			

microscopic appearance

microscopic appearance

Hot Melt — Blue
SC — Orange
LC — Green
ST™-comp. — Brown
premises — Slate
singlemode — White
62.5μ
50μ

appearance with VFL

Method Style/Type	Connector Color					METHOD B INITIAL TEST SOURCE@A SOURCE @B	METHOD B TEST> REWORK SOURCE@A SOURCE @B	Appearance: Glow(G) or No Glow (NG)

appearance with VFL

Unicam® — Red
SC — Black
LC — Yellow
ST™-comp. — Violet
premises — Rose
singlemode — Aqua
62.5μ
50μ

test procedure: EIA/TIA-526-14/Method B[1 lead reference] @850 _____ 1300 _____
test procedure: single ended test to qualify reference lead @850 nm @ ≤ 0.5 dB
Note: mandrel used; Category 2 source used

Microscope @ 400x

For polish connectors
G= round, clear, featureless, flush core; clean cladding; clean ferrule surface
NG= not G

For no polish connectors   VFL at end opposite end being evaluated
Appearance with VFL: Glow(G) or No Glow (NG)

Range Calculation

Measurement #	Source at End A both ends	Source at End B both ends
1		
2		
3		
4		
5		
6		

Largest= [   ] [   ]

Smallest= [   ] [   ]

Difference= [   ] [   ]

enter the larger
of the differences = [   ]

Maximum   #   @

cable   [   ] X [   ] = [   ]

connector   [   ] X [   ] = [   ]

splice   [   ] X [   ] = [   ]   **Maximum Loss**

[   ]

Typical

cable   [   ] X [   ] = [   ]

connector   [   ] X [   ] = [   ]

splice   [   ] X [   ] = [   ]   **Typical Loss**

[   ]

add and divide by 2

Insertion losss acceptance value= [   ]

OTDR acceptance values

Attenuation rate   [   ] + [   ] /2= [   ] dB/km +uniform loss

Connector loss   [   ] + [   ] /2= [   ] db/pair

splice   [   ] + [   ] /2= [   ] db/splice

Certificaton Exercise 19.7.2

	#		@			

Maximum

cable ☐ X ☐ = ☐

connector ☐ X ☐ = ☐

splice ☐ X ☐ = ☐   **Maximum Loss**
☐

Typical

cable ☐ X ☐ = ☐

connector ☐ X ☐ = ☐

splice ☐ X ☐ = ☐   **Typical Loss**
☐

add and divide by 2

Insertion losss acceptance value= ☐

OTDR acceptance values

Attenuation rate ☐ + ☐ /2= ☐ dB/km +uniform loss

Connector loss ☐ + ☐ /2= ☐ db/pair

splice ☐ + ☐ /2= ☐ db/splice

Safety Rules
For Fiber Optics

- Keep all food and beverages out of the work area. If fiber particles are ingested they can cause internal hemorrhaging.

- Always wear safety glasses with side shields to protect your eyes from fiber shards or splinters. Treat fiber optic splinters the same as you would treat glass splinters.

- Keep track of all fiber and cable scraps and dispose of them properly. If available, work on black work mats and wear disposable lab aprons to minimize fiber particles on your clothing. Fiber particles on your clothing can later get into food, drinks, and/or be ingested by other means.

- Never look directly into the end of fiber cables – especially with a microscope - until you are positive that there is no light source at the other end – having tested it with a power meter. Use a fiber optic power meter to make certain the fiber is dark. When using an optical tracer or continuity checker, look at the fiber from an angle at least 6 inches away from your eye to determine if the visible light is present..

- Contact lens wearers must not handle their lenses until they have thoroughly washed their hands.

- Do not touch your eyes while working with fiber optic systems until your hands have been thoroughly washed.

- Only work in well-ventilated areas.

- Keep all combustible materials safely away from the curing ovens and fusion splicers.

- When finished with the lab, dispose of all scraps properly. Put all fiber scraps in a properly marked container for disposal.

- Thoroughly clean your work area when you are done.

For more information on Safety, see the FOA Online Reference Guide / Safety

The Fiber Optic Association, Inc.
1119 S. Mission Road #355, Fallbrook, CA 92028
1-760-451-3655 Fax 1-781-207-2421
Email: info@thefoa.org   http://www.TheFOA.org

The Fiber Optic Association, Inc.

1119 S. Mission Road #355, Fallbrook, California 92028 USA
1-760-451-3655 Fax 1-781-207-2421
Email: info@thefoa.org   http://www.TheFOA.org

The Fiber Optic Association CFOT Application
For students at FOA Approved Schools

You must include a valid mailing address to receive your FOA credentials!
Your certification is not valid until you receive your ID card from FOA.

School Name_Pearson Technologies Inc._____School #_1010____Date_____

CFOT Number 1010_____ (*to be assigned by school*) Test Score _____

Name_____Title_____

Company_____*Include only if mailing address is to company!*

Street_____[ ] home [ ] business address

City_____State/Prov._____

Zip/Post. Code_____ Country _____

Phone_____Fax_____

email_____

Applicant Profile:
Business Type (check one):
[ ] Installer/contractor
[ ] FO Consultant
[ ] Commercial End user :
   Industry_____
[   ]Number of years experience in fiber optics

[ ] Military end user
[ ] Employed in FO industry
   Job function_____
[ ] Instructor/teacher
[ ] Trade press/Writer

Certification Terms and Conditions:
By this application, I attest that I have achieved a satisfactory grade on the FOA CFOT exam and apply for CFOT Certification. I certify that the information I have provided on this application is complete and accurate to the best of my knowledge. I understand that any certification granted by The FOA does not consititute licensure to practice or provide services when required by any relevant law. I understand The FOA certification does not in any way imply that The FOA assumes responsibility or liability for my actions, and I hereby indemnify The FOA from any liability resulting from my actions.

Signature _____Date _____

Instructor ___Eric R. Pearson_____CFOT# __005_____

Student Must Be Given Receipt For Exam – Page 2

NAME: _____   **EXAM ID :** _____

1	34	67	101
2	35	68	102
3	36	69	103
4	37	70	104
5	38	71	105
6	39	72	106
7	40	73	107
8	41	74	108
9	42	75	109
10	43	76	110
11	44	77	111
12	45	78	112
13	46	79	113
14	47	80	114
15	48	81	115
16	49	82	116
17	50	83	117
18	51	84	118
19	52	85	119
20	53	86	120
21	54	87	
22	55	88	
23	56	89	
24	57	90	
25	58	91	
26	59	92	
27	60	93	
28	61	94	
29	62	95	
30	63	96	
31	64	97	
32	65	98	
33	66	99	
		100	

EXAMINATION ANSWER SHEET

www.ingramcontent.com/pod-product-compliance
Lightning Source LLC
Chambersburg PA
CBHW060505060326
40689CB00020B/4644